THE FRENCH CLASSROOM

IS BUZZING

This book is a resource for fabulous teachers of French looking for supplemental task-oriented activities for beginners of French.

The guided activities in this book allow students to perform real-life and realistic tasks that are aligned with AP and IB philosophies.

Tips for teachers and students facilitate instructional planning.

Essential questions that accompany the theme-based activities target a realistic focus and context.

CONTENTS

The French Classroom is Buzzing
Guided Tasks and Activities
for Beginning Learners of French

Objective 1: give students of French regular opportunities to practice tasks that line up with the AP French Language and Culture Exam right from the very beginning stages of their French studies.

Process: use a workbook with contextualized and thematically-based tasks that are incremental baby steps toward AP exam tasks such as *e-mail writing, conversation and cultural comparison.*

Objective 2: give students of French regular opportunities to practice tasks that line up with the DP French B Exam right from the very beginning stages of their French studies.

Process: use a workbook with contextualized and thematically-based tasks that are incremental baby steps toward DP exam tasks such as *oral interactive activities, presentational activities and visual interpretation.*

Why did I write this manual?

My leitmotiv over the years has always been to prepare students thoroughly in the beginning levels of French to facilitate a smooth transition into advanced courses. The concept of reverse design is always on my mind when I start teaching a beginning course: I look at my beginners as embryos who will grow and mature under my nurturing and loving care. What an amazing honor, responsibility and challenge it is to instill into the youngest of our students the love of learning a language and a culture!

After teaching all levels of French in the Miami Public Schools for 27 years, I currently teach two beginning level classes along with a higher level course at DCC-HS, an International Baccalaureate school in Colorado Springs; in my advanced course, I teach both the Advanced Placement and Diploma Years International Baccalaureate programs. This can be a challenging situation but, once again, I note that students with a strong and well-balanced foundation make my job easier as I guide them through both programs.

In this manual, I am sharing strategies and activities that can be used in the first few years of high school French to give students a strong foundation regardless of whether their studies culminate in the DP or AP exams.

Content of this manual
Interpersonal and presentational writing-speaking activities in beginning French classes to supplement or accompany any textbook

In order to prepare students for a successful AP or DP experience, teachers must develop and implement sound instructional strategies and activities throughout the years leading up to the actual exam year. There is now a variety of excellent textbooks in use. However, teachers must still master the art of facilitating and supporting activities that will incrementally lead students to perform specific tasks in a variety of contexts. In this manual, teachers can find instructional strategies and activities that can be used in the beginning stages of French language and culture acquisition for conversation, e-mail writing and cultural comparison.

This manual contains 5 thematic units for a French level 1 course and 5 thematic units for a French level 2 course. Each unit includes performance objectives, essential questions, and detailed activities accompanied by prompts, instructions, tips to students, tips to teachers for the following communicative tasks:

1. Guided interpersonal and presentational oral communication

2. Guided interpersonal and presentational written communication

3. Oral or written cultural comparisons

4. Projects

5. Formative and summative performance activities

The pictures that appear in the appendix are clip art and free google photos; they are merely ideas to prompt students to speak and make cultural comparisons. Teachers are encouraged to use better quality authentic photos from their textbooks

Similarities and differences in the

French Language and Culture Advanced Placement Course

and the

French B International Diploma Years Course

My comments and opinions are based on my experience, having taught AP for over thirty years and DP for the last seven years.
Eliane Kurbegov

At the heart of the IB philosophy and mission are individual reflection, international awareness and action.

At the heart of the AP philosophy and mission are the development of critical thinking and access to rigorous course content for all students.

ACTFL's **Standards for Foreign language Learning,** otherwise known as the **5 Cs** [Communication, Cultures, Connections, Comparisons and Communities] are relevant in today's classroom regardless of whether a school favors the IB or AP philosophy. Best practices for teaching a world language in the 21st century revolve around these five concepts and practices.

Similarities

Both programs require a theme-based curriculum: An AP course covers 6 overarching themes while a DP course covers had 3 core themes and two optional themes.

AP themes	DP themes
Global challenges	Global issues-Core
Families and Communities	Social Relationships-Core
Beauty and Aesthetics	Communication and Media-Core
Personal and Public Identities	Cultural Diversity/Customs and Traditions
Contemporary Life	Leisure/Health
Science and Technology	Science and Technology
*Each unit comprises **essential questions***	*Each unit comprises **guiding questions***
*AP themes are taught within specific **contexts***	*DP themes are taught with a focus on specific **aspects***

Both programs promote communication in the 6 following modes:

AP modes	DP modes
Interpretational written and audio	Interpretational written and visual
Interpersonal written and spoken	Interpersonal written and spoken
Presentational written and spoken	Presentational written and spoken

Both programs rely on a variety of sources (authentic written and audio sources in AP - authentic written and visual sources in DP).

AP sources	DP sources
Written (variety of authentic printed texts including graphs) for interpretational communication	Written (variety of authentic printed texts)
Audio (variety of authentic audio texts including interviews, radio announcements and advertisements) for interpretational communication	
Guided oral interactions based on written outline and oral prompts	Authentic oral interactions provided by teacher and peers in the classroom
Combination of authentic printed and audio sources for interpretational communication	Authentic visuals for oral presentational and interactive communication
Combination of authentic printed and audio sources for persuasive written communication	Authentic printed texts selected by students for written presentational communication

Differences

The two programs present significant differences in their evaluation processes.

The AP evaluation is one single exam to be evaluated and scored externally. It …

- tests students' understanding of authentic **print and audio** sources intended for a wide range of audiences
- tests students' ability to analyze authentic **print and audio** sources from various French-speaking regions in the world
- tests students' skills to communicate in speaking and writing in the interpersonal mode (structured - specific prompts)
- tests students' skills to communicate in speaking and writing in the presentational mode (structured - specific prompts)
- tests students' understanding of cultural facets (perspectives, products, practices with regards to art, education, politics, entertainment, technology, media etc.) in various French-speaking regions in the world

The DP evaluation includes an exam to be evaluated and scored externally in addition to an internal assessment by the classroom teacher (interactive oral), an oral presentation followed by a discussion between teacher and student assessed internally (visual interpretation), and a written production supervised by the teacher but assessed externally (intertextual analysis based on authentic texts selected by the student). It …

- tests students' understanding of authentic **print** sources intended for a wide range of audiences
- tests students' ability to analyze authentic **print** sources from various French-speaking regions in the world
- tests students' skills in inter-textual analysis (authentic print sources)
- tests students' skills to communicate in speaking and writing in the interpersonal mode (some flexibility in choosing content through a choice of prompts and formats)
- tests students' skills to communicate in speaking and writing in the presentational mode (some flexibility in choosing content through a choice of prompts or presentational formats)
- tests students' understanding of cultural facets (perspectives, products, practices with regards to art, education, politics, entertainment, technology, media etc.) in various French-speaking regions in the world

Conclusions

1. In an AP course, students must have practiced listening skills with authentic audio sources (Radio-TV-podcasts) in order to be prepared for the AP examination. The DP program does not test listening skills in that manner. Rather, listening skills are assessed in interpersonal conversations (student to student and student to teacher). That being said, a well-balanced curriculum will allow students to practice with audio sources regardless of whether this specific task in on the examination.

2. Prompts for speaking and writing are specific in AP while offering some choice in DP. This may appear to favor DP students. However, DP students must use good judgment when choosing their prompt and, for the writing, must be well versed in in different styles for different audiences.

3. Although the day to day teaching and learning itself, in AP or DP, should be based on best practices and authentic resources, *it is essential that students have the opportunity to practice the specific tasks of their respective exams throughout the year since the exam formats are quite different.*

4. Both courses require students to demonstrate interpretational and communicative proficiency in reading, listening, speaking and writing as well as an ability to think critically.

5. Both courses require that students be able to compare cultures in the target language. However, one of the Free Response tasks on the AP French exam calls on students to demonstrate specific cultural knowledge and compare specific cultural practices.

My supplemental resources
- o L'alphabet et les accents/ La prononciation : *French for Dummies or French Conversation Demystified/McGrawHill*
- o Les conjugaisons/ Les genres et les accords : *Grammar Drills/McGrawHill*
- o Le vocabulaire: *Basic French/McGrawHill*

Unit 1

Family and Friends / La famille et les amis

> *The 3 modes of communication*
> - *Interpretive (print, visual and audio-visual)*
> - *Interpersonal (writing and speaking to one another)*
> - *Presentational (oral and written)*

Theme: (AP)Family and community/(DP)Social Relationships

A. Performance Objectives

- Interpret short authentic passages that are in the target language [print, audio, audio-visual] and that are related to family and friends in parts of the francophone world
- Describe and discuss friends and family in the interpersonal and presentational modes of communication.

B. Essential Questions

1. **Comment peut-on définir une famille? Dans quelle mesure les animaux et les amis font-ils partie de la famille?**

2. **Quelles similarités et quelles différences trouve-t-on dans la structure de la famille à travers diverses cultures?**

Inquiry statement: Le soutien moral qu'un individu trouve dans la famille et parmi les amis semble essentiel au développement et à l'équilibre psychique [à travers le monde et depuis tout temps].

C. Interpretive communication activities

1. Reading-group and individual with authentic print resources [text/text with pictures]
2. Listening: to the instructor and/or peers
3. Listening to authentic audio/audio-visual material [simple news, videos, songs, movie excerpts etc

D. Interpersonal communication activities

1. Speaking - paired activity

Examples of instructions and focused context for a guided conversation

Parlez à un(e) camarade de classe de votre famille. Vous allez décrire un ou deux membres de votre famille.	Parlez à un(e) camarade de classe de vos amis. Vous allez décrire un(e) ami(e). Vous allez aussi mentionner une ou deux choses que vous faites ensemble.
<ul><li>*portrait physique*</li><li>*âge*</li><li>*quelques traits de personnalité*</li><li>*activités favorites*</li><li>*occupations*</li></ul>	<ul><li>*portrait physique*</li><li>*âge*</li><li>*quelques traits de personnalité*</li><li>*vie scolaire*</li><li>*activités de loisirs favorites*</li><li>*activités que vous faites ensemble*</li></ul>

Tips to students	Tips to teachers
<ul><li>Be sure to listen carefully to your friend and react to what they say either by answering questions they pose or interjecting surprise, regret, happiness etc.</li><li>Ask for clarification by posing direct questions or repeating what you may have understood.</li><li>Use transitions that make sense in the context. Do not jump to another topic without a logical reason for it.</li><li>Show curiosity and interest in what your friend says.</li></ul>	<ul><li>Be sure to monitor the various pairs of students and give them feedback.</li><li>Do not provide vocabulary. Encourage students to use what they already know rather than repeating things they will not remember.</li><li>Teach students coordinating conjunctions like **mais, et, car, parce que** as well as interjections like **Vraiment, Pas possible, Tu blagues** and question words like **Qui, Comment, Quand** and **Pourquoi**. All these will allow students to provide and ask for details.</li></ul>

2. Writing -answering an e-mail

Prompts, instructions and tips for an e-mail response

> ➢ **Ecrivez un courriel à un correspondant. Présentez-vous ainsi que votre famille.**
> ➢ **Ecrivez un courriel à un correspondant. Décrivez un(e) ami(e).**

Tips to students

- **Use the familiar register since you're writing to a friend.**
- Be sure to open and close your message appropriately (**Cher/Chère, Au revoir/Salut**).
- Say some things that are unique and interesting with the language you have learned.
- Ask some questions (**où, quand, qui, comment**).
- Use coordinating words (**et, mais**).
- Show curiosity and interest in what your friend says (**chouette, cool, Ah bon**).

Tips to teachers

- Have students write and respond to one another within the same class or between same level classes.
- Teach students opening and closing terms like **Cher/Chère, Au revoir/Salut.**
- Be sure to monitor the writing of students. Encourage them to edit their work.
- Do not provide vocabulary except for idioms. Encourage students to use what they already know.
- Remind students to use coordinating conjunctions like **mais** and **et** as well as interjections like **chouette, cool, Ah bon** and question words like **où, quand, qui, comment.**
- Give students the list of *Tips for students* as a rubric.

Note: a laminated poster featuring question words and key coordinating words can be displayed permanently in the classroom and regularly referenced.

E. Presentational communication activities

Written: posters, brochures

> *Example of a prompt for a poster:*
>
> Comment est un vrai ami selon toi ? Chaque adjectif qui décrit ton ami doit être accompagné d'un exemple et d'une image.

Oral (make a recording of a phone or personal invitation) or *written* (e-mail/card): invitations

> *Example of a prompt for an invitation:*
>
> Invite un copain ou une copine à ta fête d'anniversaire. Indique la date de la fête, l'heure et le lieu, et aussi le nombre de personnes que tu invites.

Oral or written: visual Interpretation

> *Example of instructions for a visual interpretation exercise based on the photo of a French family having a picnic on the lawn near a castle or in a public park:*
>
> Décrivez l'image: le nombre de personnes, leurs âges, où ils sont. Exprimez des opinions (justifiez-les autant que possible) :
> - Ce sont des amis ou des membres d'une famille ?
> - C'est le week-end ou la semaine ?
> - C'est en France ou aux États-Unis ?

Oral or written: cultural comparison

> *Instructions for a cultural comparison exercise based on the picture of a French family having a picnic (same picture as in previous activity) and that of an American family having a picnic.*
>
> Comparez les deux photos: le nombre de personnes, leurs âges, où ils sont. Exprimez des opinions et justifiez-les autant que possible.

F. Projects

The following activities allow students to do their own research based on personal interest and practice written and oral presentational skills.

1. Formative activity (the activity should be written and edited, as well as practiced orally)

- Décrivez et comparez les drapeaux de 3 pays francophones (les couleurs, le dessin, les images).
- Décrivez et comparez les traits géographiques de 3 pays francophones (reliefs, paysages, climat, continent).
- Comparez la population de 3 pays francophones (dire et écrire les chiffres).

2. Summative activity (oral or written)

Présentez un pays francophone à votre classe à l'aide d'un poster ou d'une brochure. Faites attention d'inclure les choses suivantes :

- Une carte du pays avec son nom français, sa capitale, deux traits géographiques principaux ou notables (mer, océan, montagne, fleuve ...)
- Le nom du continent où le pays se trouve
- Sa population
- Le drapeau du pays avec sa description en français

> Exemple de critères de notation
>
> 1. Le contenu est complet.
> 2. Les renseignements requis sont en français compréhensible.
> 3. Les faits sont corrects.
> 4. Les noms propres sont épelés correctement.
> 5. La présentation visuelle du poster ou de la brochure est propre, clairement organisée et soignée.

Level 1 - Unit 2

Daily Life

La vie de tous les jours

The 3 modes of communication

- *Interpretive (print, visual and audio-visual)*
- *Interpersonal (writing and speaking to one another)*
- *Presentational (oral and written)*

Theme: (AP) Family and Community/(DP)Social Relationships

A. Performance Objectives

- Interpret short authentic passages that are in the target language [print, audio, audio-visual] and that are related to daily activities such as going to school, playing sports, eating at home and going out with friends and family, in parts of the francophone world.
- Describe and discuss daily activities performed at various moments in time (weekdays, weekends, summer, winter, morning, evening etc.) and in various places (home, school) in the interpersonal and presentational modes of communication.

B. Essential Questions

1. En quoi consiste une vie bien équilibrée?
2. Comment balancez-vous le travail et les loisirs?

Inquiry statement: Le travail et les loisirs sont deux façons très différentes de passer son temps. Certaines personnes trouvent plus de plaisir dans l'un ou l'autre de ces aspects du temps; d'autres équilibrent bien les deux.

C. Interpretive communication activities

1. Reading-group and individual with authentic print resources [text/text with pictures]
2. Listening: to the instructor and/or peers
3. Listening to authentic audio/audio-visual material [simple news, videos, songs, movie excerpts etc.]

D. Interpersonal communication activities

Note: I chose to give instructions to students in the familiar register for this unit.

1. **Speaking - paired activity**

   ➢ **Prompts, instructions and tips for a guided conversation**

Parle à un(e) camarade de classe d'une journée typique en semaine.	Parle à un(e) camarade de classe de votre week-end.
• *l'heure des repas* • *les cours et es devoirs* • *les activités scolaires* • *les sports* • *la télévision, le portable, les jeux*	• *l'heure des repas* • *les sorties en famille* • *les sorties avec les amis* • *les sports et les randonnées* • *la télévision et les passe-temps*

Tips to students	Tips to teachers
• Be sure to listen carefully to your friends and react to what they say either by answering questions they pose or interjecting surprise, regret, happiness etc. • Ask for clarification by posing direct questions or repeating what you may have understood. • Use transitions that make sense in the context. Do not jump to another topic without a logical reason for it. • Show curiosity and interest in what your friend says.	• Be sure to monitor the various pairs of students and give them feedback. • Do not provide vocabulary. Encourage students to use what they already know. • Remind students to use coordinating conjunctions like **mais, et, car, parce que** as well as interjections like **Vraiment, Pas possible, Tu blagues.** Also remind them to ask questions like **où, qui, comment, quand** and **pourquoi.** All these will allow students to provide and ask for details. • Encourage the use of stress pronouns (**Moi, je** or **Toi, tu**) during interactions.

2. Writing - paired activity

Prompts, instructions and tips for guided interpersonal writing [e-mail, journal]

➤ **Ecris un courriel à un(e) correspondant(e). Après une petite introduction, présente-lui ta journée typique en forme de tableau.**

7h	Petit déjeuner
8h	
midi	
15h	
18h	
19h	

➤ **Lis le courriel d'un camarade et note les similarités et les différences entre vos journées typiques.**

Tips to students for writing and responding to e-mails

- Be sure to open and close your message appropriately.
- Use the familiar register since you're writing to a peer.
- Explain that you want to present your regular daily routine
- Ask some questions.
- Use transitions and interjections.
- In your response (prompt 2), show curiosity and interest in what your friend says.
- Note a difference in your schedule and your friend's.

Tips to teachers

- Have students write and respond to one another within the same class or between same level classes
- Teach/Remind students opening and closing terms like **Cher/Chère** and **A+.**
- Be sure to monitor the writing of students. Encourage them to edit their work.
- Do not provide vocabulary except for idioms. Encourage students to use what they already know.
- Remind students to use coordinating conjunctions like **mais**, **et**, **car**, **parce que** as well as interjections like **Crois-moi** or **Je t'assure** and question words like **Qui**, **Comment**, **Quand** and **Pourquoi**.
- Give students the list of *Tips for students* as a rubric and hold them accountable.

E. Presentational communication activities

Written: posters, brochures, journals

> *Example of a prompt for a journal:*

> Note les similarités et les différences entre ta journée typique et la journée typique de ton/ta camarade. Par exemple, *Michel et moi, nous avons le petit déjeuner à 7h et le déjeuner à midi.*

Oral: recording

> *Example of instructions and prompt for a recorded presentation:*

> Prépare un enregistrement pour un correspondant francophone. Mentionne combien de temps tu consacres à tes activités scolaires et à tes activités de loisirs et quand tu fais ces activités.

Oral or written: visual interpretation

> *Example of instructions for a visual interpretation exercise based on the photo of French teenagers leaving school at 5 pm.*

> Décris l'image: qui, quel âge, où, à quelle heure. Exprime des opinions (et justifie si tu peux) : c'est un jeune Français ou un jeune Américain ? C'est le week-end ou la semaine ? C'est en France ou aux États-Unis ?

Oral or written: Cultural comparison

> *Example of instructions for a cultural comparison exercise based on the photo of French teenagers leaving school at 5 pm. (same picture as in previous activity) and that of an American high school with passing of classes and emphasis on football.*

> Compare les deux photos: qui, quel âge, où, à quelle heure. Exprime des opinions sur la durée et la structure de la journée scolaire.

F. Projects

The following activities allow students to do their own research based on personal interest and practice written and oral presentational skills.

1. Formative activity (the activity has to be written and edited, as well as practiced orally)

- Compare la journée scolaire d'un lycéen québécois ou français avec celle d'un lycéen américain. Utilise des dessins ou des diagrammes.

- Montre graphiquement combien de temps tu consacres au travail scolaire et aux loisirs. Utilise des dessins ou des diagrammes.

2. Summative activity (oral or written)

Présente ta journée typique en semaine ou le week-end à l'aide d'une bande dessinée que tu vas créer (illustrations et textes). Fais attention d'inclure les choses suivantes :

- Ton nom
- Ton âge
- Une date
- Différents moments de la journée
- Des activités diverses (travail/loisirs)

Exemple de critères de notation

1. Le contenu (texte et dessins) est approprié.

2. Les renseignements requis sont en français compréhensible.

3. Le texte est clair et organisé.

4. Les noms propres sont épelés correctement.

5. La présentation visuelle de la BD est propre, clairement organisée, conforme au format BD.

Unit 3

City Living /La vie urbaine

> **The 3 modes of communication**
>
> - *Interpretive (print, visual and audio-visual)*
> - *Interpersonal (writing and speaking to one another)*
> - *Presentational (oral and written)*

Theme: (AP)Contemporary Life/(DP)Cultural Diversity

A. Performance Objectives

- Interpret short authentic passages that are in the target language [print, audio, audio-visual] and that are related to city living and transportation, in parts of the francophone world.
- Describe and discuss various types of lodging (house and apartment with rooms, furnishings etc.) and various types of transportation (bike, bus, train, car, subway) in the interpersonal and presentational modes of communication.

B. Essential Questions

1. Pourquoi aimez-vous ou n'aimez-vous pas vivre en ville?
2. Quelle diversité trouve-t-on dans votre ville?

Inquiry statement: La population qui regroupe les jeunes familles et les immigrants est de plus en plus concentrée dans les grands centres urbains. C'est un phénomène mondial.

C. Interpretive communication activities

1. Reading-group and individual with authentic print resources [text/text with pictures]
2. Listening: to the instructor and/or peers
3. Listening to authentic audio/audio-visual material [simple news, videos, songs, movie excerpts etc.]

D. Interpersonal communication activities

1. Speaking - paired activity
  ➢ **Prompts, instructions and tips for a guided conversation**

Parlez avec un(e) camarade de classe de votre maison ou de votre appartement. Prétendez que le/la camarade ne connaît pas votre logement ou votre maison.	Parlez avec un(e) camarade de classe de votre logement ou de votre maison. Prétendez que le/la camarade vient d'arriver et ne connaît pas encore la ville.
• *où je fais ma toilette* • *où je mange* • *où je regarde la télé* • *où je fais les devoirs* • *ma chambre et mes effets personnels*	• *comment je vais à l'école* • *comment je vais au cinéma avec des amis* • *comment je retrouve des amis* • *comment je rends visite à des membres de la famille*

Tips to students	Tips to teachers
• Be sure to listen carefully to your friends and react to what they say either by answering questions they pose or interjecting surprise, regret, happiness etc. • Ask for clarification by posing direct questions or repeating what you may have understood. • Use transitions that make sense in the context. Do not jump to another topic without a logical reason for it. • Show curiosity and interest in what your friend says. • Use stress pronouns when appropriate. • Vary the manner in which you question and the manner in which you show interest, surprise etc. • Use adjectives and adverbs to enrich communication.	• Be sure to monitor the various pairs of students and give them feedback. • Encourage students to use what they already know. • Remind students to use coordinating conjunctions like **mais, et, car, parce que** as well as interjections like **Vraiment, Pas possible, Tu blagues.** Also remind them to ask questions like **Qui, Comment, Quand** and **Pourquoi.** All these will allow students to provide and ask for details. • Encourage the use of stress pronouns (**Moi, je** or **Toi, tu**) during interactions. • Encourage students to vary vocabulary and structures. • Encourage the use of adjectives and commonly used adverbs (**ici, là-bas, déjà, aussi, alors**...)

2. Writing - answering an e-mail

Prompt, instructions and tips for an e-mail response

> ➤ **Répondez au courriel de votre correspondant. Répondez à ses questions et posez-lui aussi une question.**

Cher Marc,

Tu sais que j'habite à Strasbourg. C'est une grande ville près de l'Allemagne. Beaucoup de gens ici parlent français et allemand. Il y a aussi des immigrés du Maghreb et d'Afrique. Est-ce que tu parles anglais et espagnol où tu habites ? Est-ce que ta ville est grande ou petite ? Il y a combien de personnes qui habitent là-bas ? De quelles origines sont-elles ? Quelles langues parlent-elles ?

A +
Francine

Tips to students for responding to e-mails in the familiar register

- Be sure to open your message and close your message appropriately.

- Answer this e-mail in the familiar register.
- Answer the questions asked by your correspondent.
- Organize your ideas using paragraphs, using indentations and appropriate conventions.
- Show curiosity and interest in what your correspondent says and ask him/her to clarify or expand.

Tips to teachers

- Have students write and respond to one another within the same class or between same level classes.
- Remind students to use opening and closing terms like **Cher/Chère** and **A+.**
- Be sure to monitor the writing of students. Encourage them to edit their work.
- Encourage students to use what they already know and have recently learned.
- Remind students to use coordinating conjunctions like **mais, et, car, parce que** as well as interjections like **Crois-moi** or **Je t'assure** and question words like **Où, Qui, Comment, Quand** and **Pourquoi.**
- Encourage students to use subject and stress pronouns as well as adjectives and adverbs to enrich their written communication.
- Give students the list of *Tips to students* as a rubric and hold them accountable.

E. Presentational communication activities

Written: poster or brochure

Dessinez une rue typique dans votre ville ou dans une ville que vous connaissez. Vous pouvez inclure des magasins, des restaurants, un arrêt de métro, une banque, une poste etc. Indiquez les noms de ces endroits.

Oral: recording

Example: local TV channel reporter   rush hour coverage

Vous êtes reporter pour une chaîne locale et vous commentez ce qui se passe dans votre ville aux informations de cinq heures.

Oral or written: visual Interpretation

Example of instructions for a visual interpretation exercise based on the photo of a Francophone high school student taking the city bus to go to school.

Décrivez l'image: qui, quel âge, où, comment? Exprimez des opinions et justifiez-les autant que possible.

Oral or written: cultural comparison

Example of instructions for a cultural comparison exercise based on the photo of a Francophone high school student taking the bus (same picture as in previous activity) and that of an American teenager driving to school.

Comparez les deux photos. Exprimez des opinions sur les différences ou les similarités entre les deux ados.

F. Projects

The following activities allow students to do their own research based on personal interest and practice written and oral presentational skills.

A. Formative activity (the activity has to be written and edited, as well as practiced orally)

- Trouvez une photo sur internet d'un quartier de votre ville (ou d'une ville proche) et identifiez les endroits principaux (hôtel de ville, musée, centre commercial, université etc.). Ajoutez un petit texte descriptif.

- Trouvez une photo sur internet d'un quartier dans une grande ville francophone. Reproduisez-la photo et écrivez un petit texte descriptif.

B. Summative activity

- Comparez un quartier urbain dans une région francophone avec un quartier urbain dans votre communauté. Utilisez des dessins ou des diagrammes avec de brefs textes descriptifs.

- Comparez un appartement urbain dans une région francophone avec un appartement urbain dans votre communauté. Utilisez des dessins ou des diagrammes avec de brefs textes descriptifs.

Exemple de critères de notation

1. Les faits et les photos (dessins) correspondent aux instructions.
2. Le vocabulaire du texte est approprié et varié pour ce niveau.
3. Les structures sont correctes.
4. Les noms propres sont épelés correctement.
5. La présentation visuelle est propre, clairement organisée et

---

Level 1 - Unit 4

Free Time/Les loisirs et les passe-temps

> *The 3 modes of communication*
> - *Interpretive (print, visual and audio-visual)*
> - *Interpersonal (writing and speaking to one another)*
> - *Presentational (oral and written)*

Theme: (AP)Beauty and Aesthetics/(DP)Leisure

A. Performance Objectives

- Interpret short authentic passages that are in the target language [print, audio, audio-visual] and that are related to free time activities, in parts of the francophone world.

- Describe and discuss various ways of enjoying free time (crafts, sports, TV and cinema, internet, music, shopping) in the interpersonal and presentational modes of communication.

B. Essential Questions

1. **Quelles activités vous font plaisir et vous aident à décompresser ?**

2. **Pourquoi est-il important d'avoir des passe-temps ?**

Inquiry statement: Les passe-temps comme les sports, les jeux, la lecture, les activités médiatiques ont pour but d'améliorer la qualité de la vie. Il est pourtant possible de passer de la passion à la dépendance.

C. Interpretive communication activities

4. Reading-group and individual with authentic print resources [text/text with pictures]

5. Listening: to the instructor and/or peers

6. Listening to authentic audio/audio-visual material [simple news, videos, songs, movie excerpts etc.]

D. Interpersonal communication activities

1. Speaking - paired activity

➢ Prompts, instructions and tips for a guided conversation

Parlez avec un(e) camarade de classe de ce que vous faites le week-end.	Parlez avec un(e) camarade de classe de vos interactions liées aux nouvelles technologies (portable, ordi etc.).
• *mes activités le week-end* • *ce que je regarde à la télé ou au cinéma* • *mes activités sportives* • *ma musique* • *mes lectures*	• *mon cellulaire* • *mon internet* • *mes réseaux sociaux* • *mes jeux*

Tips to students	Tips to teachers
• Be sure to listen carefully to your friends and react to what they say either by answering questions they pose or interjecting surprise, regret, happiness etc. • Ask for clarification by posing direct questions or repeating what you may have understood. • Use transitions that make sense in the context. Do not jump to another topic without a logical reason for it. • Show curiosity and interest in what your friend says. • Use stress pronouns when appropriate. • Vary the manner in which you question and the manner in which you show interest, surprise etc. • Use adjectives and adverbs to enrich communication. • Compare what your friends do with what you do.	• Be sure to monitor the various pairs of students and give them feedback. • Encourage students to use what they already know. • Remind students to use coordinating conjunctions like **mais**, **et**, **car**, **parce que** as well as interjections like **Vraiment**, **Pas possible**, **Tu blagues**. Also remind them to ask questions like **Qui**, **Comment**, **Quand** and **Pourquoi**. All these will allow students to provide and ask for details. • Encourage the use of stress pronouns (**Moi, je** or **Toi, tu**) during interactions. • Encourage students to vary vocabulary and structures. • Encourage the use of adjectives and commonly used adverbs (**ici, là-bas, déjà, aussi, alors**...). • Encourage well-developed and compound sentences.

2. Writing - answering an e-mail

Prompt, instructions and tips for an e-mail response

> ➤ **Répondez au courriel de votre correspondant. Répondez à ses questions et posez-lui aussi une ou deux questions.**

Chère Irène,

Cette semaine, j'ai un weekend de trois jours je n'ai pas cours vendredi. L'école est fermée à l'occasion de la Toussaint. Est-ce qu'il y a cette fête chez toi ?

Ma famille va rendre visite à ma grand-mère qui habite près de chez nous. Je vais revoir mes cousins et nous allons jouer au foot sur le terrain derrière la maison de grand-mère. Qu'est-ce que tu fais, toi, quand tu as un grand weekend comme ça?

A bientôt,
Luc

Tips to students for writing and responding to e-mails
- Be sure to open and close your message appropriately.
- Answer this e-mail in the familiar register.
- Answer the questions asked by your correspondent.
- Organize your ideas using paragraphs, indentations and appropriate conventions.
- Show curiosity and interest in what your correspondent says and ask him/her to clarify or expand on something.

Tips to teachers
- Remind students opening the opening terms **Cher/Chère.** Introduce closing terms like **A bientôt, salut, bises, bisous.**
- Be sure to monitor the writing of students. Encourage them to edit their work
- Encourage students to use what they already know.
- Remind students to use coordinating conjunctions like **mais, et, car, parce que** as well as interjections like **Crois-moi** or **Je t'assure** and question words like **Qui, Comment, Quand** and **Pourquoi.**
- Encourage the use of well-developed compound sentences and monitor the use of appropriate conventions (punctuation, indentation, capitalization).
- Give students the list of *Tips to students* as a rubric and hold them accountable

E. Presentational communication activities

Written: comic strip

Créez une bande dessinée de 5 images où votre personnage fait ses activités favorites du dimanche. Chaque image est sous-titrée d'un court texte.

Oral: recording

Faites un enregistrement pour votre correspondant. Mentionnez ce que vous faites généralement le weekend. Parlez aussi de ce que vous allez faire l'été prochain pendant les vacances.

Oral or written: visual Interpretation

Instructions for a visual interpretation exercise based on the photo or picture of a teenager's Saturday activities (in a Francophone region).

Décrivez la photo: qui, quel âge, où, comment, avec qui, quoi. Décrivez surtout l'activité. Exprimez aussi des opinions (et justifiez autant que possible) : c'est un jeune Français, un jeune Québécois ou un jeune Africain ?

Oral or written: Cultural comparison

Instructions for a cultural comparison exercise based on the photo of a Francophone teenager's Saturday activities (same picture as in previous activity) and that of an American teenager involved in similar or different free time activities.

Comparez les deux photos. Exprimez des opinions sur les similitudes et les différences entre les deux.

F. Projects

The following activities allow students to do research based on personal interest and practice written and oral presentational skills.

1. Formative activity (the activity has to be written and edited, and practiced orally)

- Comparez les passe-temps d'un lycéen Québécois/français/belge/suisse/africain et celles d'un lycéen américain. Utilisez des dessins ou des diagrammes sous-titrés avec un texte narratif ou explicatif.

- Montrez graphiquement comment vous passez votre temps libre. Utilisez des dessins ou des diagrammes pour illustrer et supporter votre texte.

2. Summative activity (the activity can be limited to the written product, or presented orally)

- Racontez vos activités typiques du week-end **à votre journal**. Faites attention d'inclure les aspects suivants :

  - Le format d'une lettre
  - Différents moments d'un week-end
  - Des activités de temps libre
  - Trois paragraphes distincts
  - Une variété d'adjectifs, d'adverbes et de mots-charnières
  - Une variété de verbes au présent

- Décrivez ce que vous rêvez de faire pendant les prochaines grandes vacances **à votre journal**. Faites attention d'inclure les aspects mentionnés ci-dessus, mais mettez vos verbes au **futur proche.**

> Exemple de critères de notation
>
> 1. Le format est approprié.
> 2. Le sujet est bien développé.
> 3. Les conventions sont respectées (ponctuation etc.)
> 4. Il y a une variété de vocabulaire (y compris des adjectifs, des adverbes et des mots-charnières).
> 5. La présentation est propre, clairement organisée et soignée.

Level 1 - Unit 5

At home/Chez moi

> *The 3 modes of communication*
>
> - *Interpretive (print, visual and audio-visual)*
> - *Interpersonal (writing and speaking to one another)*
> - *Presentational (oral and written)*

Theme: (AP)Beauty and Aesthetics/(DP)Leisure

A. Performance Objectives

- Interpret short authentic passages that are in the target language [print, audio, audio-visual] and that are related to free time activities, in parts of the francophone world.

- Describe and discuss various ways of enjoying free time (crafts, sports, TV and cinema, internet, music, shopping) in the interpersonal and presentational modes of communication.

B. Essential Questions

1. **What is a home?**

2. **How do you create yourself a comfortable space?**

Inquiry statement: La notion de « Chez soi » comprend l'habitation physique (maison, appartement, chambre), le lieu géographique (région, pays) ainsi que le milieu social. Finalement le « Chez soi » suggère un sens d''intimité.

C. Interpretive communication activities

1. Reading-group and individual with authentic print resources [text/text with pictures]

2. Listening: to the instructor and/or peers

3. Listening to authentic audio/audio-visual material [simple news, videos, songs, movie excerpts etc.

D. Interpersonal communication activities

1. Speaking - paired activity

> ➢ **Prompts, instructions and tips for a guided conversation**

Parlez avec un(e) camarade de classe de votre foyer.	Parlez avec un(e) camarade de classe de votre chambre.
• *où j'habite* • *ce qui rend ma maison ou mon appartement confortable* • *les endroits que je partage avec des membres de la famille* • *mon espace privé*	• *mes meubles (quoi et où)* • *mes décorations* • *mes vêtements et mes affaires personnelles* • *ma salle de bains*

Tips to students	Tips to teachers
• Be sure to listen carefully to your friends and react to what they say either by answering questions they pose or interjecting surprise, regret, happiness etc. • Ask for clarification by posing direct questions or repeating what you may have understood. • Use transitions that make sense in the context. Do not jump to another topic without a logical reason for it. • Show curiosity and interest in what your friend says. • Use stress pronouns when appropriate. • Vary the manner in which you question and the manner in which you show interest, surprise etc. • Use adjectives and adverbs to enrich communication. • Compare what your friends do with what you do.	• Be sure to monitor the various pairs of students and give them feedback. • Encourage students to use what they already know. • Remind students to use coordinating conjunctions like **mais**, **et**, **car**, **parce que** as well as interjections like **Vraiment**, **Pas possible**, **Tu blagues**. Also remind them to ask questions like **Qui**, **Comment**, **Quand** and **Pourquoi**. All these will allow students to provide and ask for details. • Encourage the use of stress pronouns (**Moi, je** or **Toi, tu**) during interactions. • Encourage students to vary vocabulary and structures. • Encourage the use of adjectives and commonly used adverbs (**ici, là-bas, déjà, aussi, alors**...). • Encourage well-developed and compound sentences.

2. Writing - answering an e-mail

Prompt, instructions and tips for an e-mail response

> ➤ **Répondez au courriel de votre correspondant. Répondez à ses questions et posez-lui aussi une ou deux questions.**

Cher Thomas,

Je suis arrivé hier au site de ma colonie de vacances (en pleine forêt montagneuse). Je loge avec trois autres gars dans une cabane en bois. Il n'y a qu'un petit salon (pas de télé), une kitchenette, une minuscule salle de bains avec douche et une chambre avec des lits superposés.

Ma chambre n'a évidemment aucun des conforts de ma chambre à la maison. Pas grave ! De toute façon je ne vais pas passer beaucoup de temps dans la cabane puisque nous allons tous les jours faire de longues randonnées.

Ce qui est magnifique ici, c'est la beauté de l'environnement. Il faut profiter de ca plutôt que de penser aux petits conforts du foyer.

Et toi, comment est-ce dans ta colo en bord de mer? Est-ce un bungalow ou une cabane comme la mienne ? Et ta chambre, comment est-elle ?

Allez, donne-moi vite de tes nouvelles, frérot.

Je t'embrasse,
Luc

Tips to students for writing and responding to e-mails

- Be sure to open and close your message appropriately.
- Answer this e-mail in the familiar register.
- Answer the questions asked by your correspondent.
- Organize your ideas using paragraphs, indentations and appropriate conventions.
- Show curiosity and interest in what your correspondent says and ask him/her to clarify or expand on something.

Tips to teachers

- Remind students opening the opening terms **Cher/Chère.** Introduce closing terms like **A bientôt, salut, bises, bisous, je t'embrasse.**
- Be sure to monitor the writing of students. Encourage them to edit their work
- Encourage students to use what they already know.
- Remind students to use coordinating conjunctions like **mais**, **et**, **car**, **parce que** as well as interjections like **Crois-moi** or **Je t'assure** and question words like **Qui**, **Comment**, **Quand** and **Pourquoi**.
- Encourage the use of well-developed compound sentences and monitor the use of appropriate conventions (punctuation, indentation, capitalization).
- Give students the list of *Tips to students* as a rubric and hold them accountable.

E. Presentational communication activities

Written: advertisement

> Créez une annonce publicitaire avec la photo et la description d'une belle maison ou d'un bel appartement à vendre.

Oral: recording

> Faites une publicité de la maison idéale pour la radio ou la télévision. Soyez imaginatif et n'omettez pas les détails uniques de cette maison.

Oral or written: visual Interpretation

> *Example of instructions for a visual interpretation exercise based on the photo of a teenager's room in a Francophone area.*
>
> Décrivez l'image: qui, quel âge, où, quelles affaires personnelles, quelles décorations ? C'est quelle pièce ? Quelle est la couleur des murs ? Exprimez des opinions et justifiez-les autant que possible : c'est un jeune Français ou un jeune Africain ?

Oral or written: cultural comparison

> *Example of instructions for a cultural comparison exercise based on the photo of a Francophone teenager in his/her room (same picture as in previous activity) and that of an American teenager in his/her room.*
>
> Comparez les deux photos. Exprimez des opinions sur les différences ou les similarités entre les deux chambres.

F. Projects

The following activities allow students to do research based on personal interest and practice written and oral presentational skills.

1. Formative activity (the activity has to be written and edited, and practiced orally)

- Comparez les passe-temps d'un lycéen Québécois/français/belge/suisse/africain et celles d'un lycéen américain. Utilisez des dessins ou des diagrammes sous-titrés avec un texte narratif ou explicatif.

- Montrez graphiquement comment vous passez votre temps libre. Utilisez des dessins ou des diagrammes pour illustrer et supporter votre texte.

2. Summative activity (the activity can be limited to the written product, or presented orally)

- Racontez vos activités typiques du week-end **à votre journal**. Faites attention d'inclure les aspects suivants :

    o   Le format d'une lettre
    o   Différents moments d'un week-end
    o   Des activités de temps libre
    o   Trois paragraphes distincts
    o   Une variété d'adjectifs, d'adverbes et de mots-charnières
    o   Une variété de verbes au présent

- Décrivez ce que vous rêvez de faire pendant les prochaines grandes vacances **à votre journal**. Faites attention d'inclure les aspects mentionnés ci-dessus, mais mettez vos verbes au **futur proche.**

> Exemple de critères de notation
>
> 1. Le format est approprié.
> 2. Le sujet est bien développé.
> 3. Les conventions sont respectées (ponctuation etc.)
> 4. Il y a une variété de vocabulaire (y compris des adjectifs, des adverbes et des mots-charnières).
> 5. La présentation est propre, clairement organisée et soignée.

Level 2 - Unit 1

Personal Identity/L'identité

> *The 3 modes of communication*
>
> - *Interpretive (print, visual and audio-visual)*
> - *Interpersonal (writing and speaking to one another)*
> - *Presentational (oral and written)*

Theme: (AP)Personal Identity/(DP)Customs and Traditions

A. Performance Objectives

- Interpret short authentic passages that are in the target language [print, audio, audio-visual] and that are related to personal identity, in parts of the francophone world.

- Describe and discuss various ways of defining personal identity (family context, nationality, cultural traits such as traditions, languages and life style, physical and personality traits, relationships) in the interpersonal and presentational modes of communication.

B. Essential Questions

1. **Qu'est-ce qui vous rend unique?**

2. **Quelle est votre place dans l'environnement social?**

Inquiry statement: Le sens identitaire change au cours du temps dû au développement physique et social de l'individu.

C. Interpretive communication activities

1. Reading-group and individual with authentic print resources [text/text with pictures]

2. Listening: to the instructor and/or peers

3. Listening to authentic audio/audio-visual material [simple news, videos, songs, movie excerpts etc.

D. Interpersonal communication activities

1. Speaking-paired activity

> #### ➤ Prompts, instructions and tips for a guided conversation

Parlez avec un(e) camarade de classe de votre personnalité et de famille.	Parlez avec un(e) camarade de classe des personnes qui jouent un rôle dans votre vie.
<ul><li>*où et quand vous êtes né(e)*</li><li>*quelle langue vous parlez en famille*</li><li>*les occupations de vos parents*</li><li>*vos traits de personnalité les plus prononcés*</li><li>*les fêtes et les traditions dans votre*</li></ul>	<ul><li>*ma famille*</li><li>*mes amis*</li><li>*mes professeurs*</li><li>*mes entraîneurs*</li><li>*mes modèles spirituels*</li></ul>

Tips to students	Tips to teachers
<ul><li>Be sure to listen carefully to your friends and react to what they say either by answering questions they pose or interjecting surprise, regret, happiness etc.</li><li>Ask for clarification by posing direct questions or repeating what you may have understood.</li><li>Ask for details [with question words such as ***comment, pourquoi, quand, avec qui, où***, or with adverbs such as ***souvent, régulièrement, jamais*** etc.].</li><li>Use transitions that make sense in the context. String your sentences logically with the appropriate *mot charnière*. Do not jump to another topic without a logical reason for it.</li><li>Show curiosity and interest in what your friend says. *Compare what they do with what you do.*</li><li>Make suggestions and express opinions.</li></ul>	<ul><li>Be sure to monitor the various pairs of students and give them feedback.</li><li>Encourage students to use what they already. Teach them to paraphrase.</li><li>Encourage students to make frequent use of transitional words or phrases such as ***alors, ainsi, ensuite, c'est pourquoi, c'est parce que, quand même, donc*** etc.</li><li>Teach students to use coordinating conjunctions like **mais, et, car, parce que** as well as interjections like **Vraiment, Pas possible, Tu blagues** and question words like **Qui, Comment, Quand, Pourquoi, Tu peux me dire.** All these will allow students to provide and ask for details.</li><li>Teach students vocabulary necessary to express opinions such as ***Moi, je pense que, A mon avis, Selon moi, Je crois que, je suis sûr(e) que***</li><li>Teach students vocabulary necessary to give advice such as ***Tu peux peut-être* + infinitive, *Je te conseille de* + infinitive, *J'espère que…***</li><li>Remind students to use adjectives and adverbs to enrich their sentences.</li></ul>

2. Writing: answering an e-mail

Prompt, instructions and tips for an e-mail response

> ➢ Répondez au courriel de votre correspondant. Répondez à ses questions et posez-lui une question aussi.

Cher Jean-Marc,

Je m'appelle Nicolas et j'ai seize ans comme toi, je crois. Je suis né à Ostwald, une petite ville en Alsace. Je parle surtout français mais je sais un peu l'allemand et je viens de commencer à étudier l'anglais.

Chez nous, en Alsace, on a des fêtes et des traditions très uniques. Par exemple, pour la Saint-Nicolas (on m'a nommé d'après ce saint), on achète ou on fait des bonhommes de pain d'épice (en anglais, c'est *gingerbread*).

Un autre exemple de quelque chose d'unique en Alsace est évident dans la photo ci-jointe où tu vois le costume folklorique de l'Alsacienne. On porte ce costume seulement pour certaines fêtes de la région.

Comment est-ce chez toi ? Quelles langues est-ce que tu apprends ? Est-ce qu'il y a des fêtes uniques comme chez nous ?

J'attends ta réponse.

Salut,

Ton nouveau copain Nicolas

Tips to students for writing and responding to e-mails

- Be sure to open and close your message appropriately.
- Answer your friend's questions.
- Show curiosity and interest in what your friend says. Ask some questions aimed at clarifications and details.
- Use paragraphs, transitions, interjections and a variety of nouns, verbs, adjectives and adverbs.
- Note some similarities and differences between your region and that of your pen pal's.

Tips to teachers

- Remind students opening and closing terms like **Cher/Chère** and **A+/A bientôt, Salut** etc.
- Be sure to monitor the writing of students. Have them edit their work.
- Encourage students to use what they already know. *Teach them the art of paraphrasing!*
- Remind students to use coordinating conjunctions like **mais**, interjections like **Crois-moi**, question words like **Pourquoi** as well as transitional words and phrases such as *C'est pourquoi*.
- Encourage students to express opinions using expressions such as **A mon avis** or **Je pense que**.
- Encourage students to explain and expand their thinking with compound sentences using terms such as **parce que** and **car**.
- Encourage students to note differences.
- Review interrogative structures (pitch of voice and *est-ce que* methods for informal register)
- Review present, near future and passé composé tenses.
- Give students the list of *Tips to students* as a rubric and hold them accountable.

E. Presentational communication activities

Written: begin a journal

> Qui suis-je ?
> Vous commencez un journal intime. Présentez-vous à votre journal comme à un(e) ami(e).

Oral: recording

> Je me présente.
> Faites un enregistrement. Mentionnez votre identité (lieu de naissance, lieu de résidence, membres de votre famille, traditions ou routines familiales, meilleurs amis).

Oral or written: visual Interpretation

> *Instructions for a visual interpretation exercise based on the photo of a teenager from a Francophone region involved in a specific family or community-related activity.*
> Décrivez la photo: quoi, qui, quel âge, où, à quelle heure. Décrivez surtout l'activité. Exprimez des opinions. Justifiez-les autant que possible.

Oral or written: Cultural comparison

> *Instructions for a cultural comparison exercise based on the previous photo and the photo of an American teenager involved in a similar or different activity.*
> Comparez les deux photos. Exprimez des opinions sur les similitudes et les différences.

F. Project

The following activities allow students to do research based on personal interest and practice written and oral presentational skills.

1. Formative activity (the activity has to be written and edited, as well as practiced orally)

- Trouvez en ligne la biographie d'un francophone célèbre (un Africain par exemple). Créez un diaporama avec quelques caractéristiques de son identité (portrait physique, occupation, personnalité, nationalité, famille, communauté).

- Faites un poster où vous vous décrivez avec autant d'adjectifs (ou de locutions adjectivales) que possible. Il faut en inclure qui vous décrivent par rapport à votre environnement. Disposez tous les adjectifs de manière originale et artistique sur le poster.

2. Summative activity: (the activity can be limited to the written product)

Dans un premier paragraphe de votre page de journal, décrivez les aspects de votre identité personnelle (et ce qui vous rend unique) à votre journal. Dans un second paragraphe, décrivez votre place dans votre famille et dans votre communauté scolaire. Faites attention d'inclure les choses suivantes :

- Le format d'une page de journal intime (comme une lettre)
- Divers aspects de votre identité (personnalité, origines et traditions ancestrales, nationalité, appartenance à des groupes particuliers, types de relations avec la famille et les amis)
- Le présent d'une variété de verbes (peut-être le futur proche et le passé composé)
- Deux paragraphes bien développés
- Des adjectifs, des adverbes et des mots charnières

Exemple de critères de notation

1. Le format est approprié.

2. Le sujet est bien développé.

3. Les conventions sont respectées (ponctuation etc.)

4. Il y a une variété de vocabulaire (y compris des adjectifs, des adverbes et des mots-charnières).

5. La présentation est propre, clairement organisée et soignée.

Level 2 - Unit 2

Social Interactions among Adolescents/La Dynamique sociale de l'Adolescent

> *The 3 modes of communication*
>
> - *Interpretive (print, visual and audio-visual)*
> - *Interpersonal (writing and speaking to one another)*
> - *Presentational (oral and written)*

Theme: (AP)Personal Identity/(DP)Social Relationships

A. Performance Objectives

- Interpret short authentic passages in the target language [print, audio, audio-visual] and that are related to social activities among adolescents, in parts of the francophone world.

- Describe and discuss various ways of defining social activities (movies, parties, video games, telephoning, e-mailing and texting) in the interpersonal and presentational modes of communication.

B. Essential Questions

1. **Quel est le rôle de vos amis dans votre vie?**

2. **Comment est-ce que les adolescents utilisent la technologie pour s'amuser, pour mieux se connaître et rester en contact?**

Inquiry statement: L'adolescent a besoin d'un cercle social (réel et virtuel) pour évoluer et grandir. Cette évolution se passe souvent dans le dialogue et la confrontation.

C. Interpretive communication activities

1. Reading-group and individual with authentic print resources [text/text with pictures]

2. Listening: to the instructor and/or peers

3. Listening to authentic audio/audio-visual material [simple news, videos, songs, movie excerpts etc.]

D. Interpersonal communication activities

1. Speaking - paired activity

Prompts, instructions and tips for a guided conversation

Parlez avec un(e) camarade de classe de vos amis.	Parlez avec un(e) camarade de classe de vos activités avec vos amis.
<ul><li>*mes amis à l'école*</li><li>*mes amis en dehors de l'école*</li><li>*les caractéristiques d'un(e) meilleur(e) ami(e)*</li></ul>	<ul><li>*le cinéma*</li><li>*les jeux vidéo*</li><li>*la communication*</li><li>*les boums*</li><li>*les sports*</li></ul>

Tips to students	Tips to teachers
<ul><li>Be sure to listen carefully to your friends and react to what they say either by answering questions they pose or interjecting surprise, regret, happiness etc.</li><li>Ask for clarification by posing direct questions or repeating what you may have understood.</li><li>Ask for details [with question words such as *comment, pourquoi, quand, avec qui, où*, or with adverbs such as *souvent, régulièrement, jamais* etc.].</li><li>Use transitions that make sense in the context. String your sentences logically with the appropriate *mot charnière*. Do not jump to another topic without a logical reason for it.</li><li>Show curiosity and interest in what your friend says. *Compare what they do with what you do.*</li><li>Make suggestions and express opinions. Justify them.</li></ul>	<ul><li>Be sure to monitor the various pairs of students and give them feedback.</li><li>Encourage students to use what they already know. Teach them to paraphrase.</li><li>Encourage students to make frequent use of transitional words or phrases such as *alors, ainsi, ensuite, c'est pourquoi, c'est parce que, quand même, donc* etc.</li><li>Teach students to use coordinating conjunctions like **mais, et, car, parce que** as well as interjections like **Vraiment, Pas possible, Tu blagues** and question words like **Qui, Comment, Quand, Pourquoi, Tu peux me dire.** All these will allow students to provide and ask for details.</li><li>Teach students vocabulary necessary to express opinions such as *Moi, je pense que, A mon avis, Selon moi, Je crois que, je suis sûr(e) que*</li><li>Teach students vocabulary necessary to give advice such as *Tu peux peut-être* + *infinitive, Je te conseille de* + *infinitive, J'espère que…*</li><li>Remind students to use adjectives and adverbs to enrich their sentences.</li></ul>

2. Writing - answering an e-mail

Prompt, instructions and tips for an e-mail response

> ➤ **Répondez au courriel de votre correspondant. Répondez à ses questions et posez-lui une question aussi.**

Chère Chloé,

Je m'appelle Suzie et j'ai quinze ans. Je suis suisse et j'habite à Lausanne.

J'ai beaucoup d'amis. Je vais à l'école tous les jours avec certains amis. Nous prenons le bus ensemble. Quelquefois, nous révisons des leçons en route. Et toi, comment tu vas à l'école et avec qui ?

Pendant la semaine, ma copine Annabelle fait souvent ses devoirs chez moi après l'école. Mes autres copines m'écrivent des texto ou des e-mails, mais maman n'aime pas que je passe trop de temps à ça.

Annabelle et moi, nous adorons regarder des vidéos sur You Tube et écouter des chansons sur nos cellulaires. Maman nous laisse faire ça après les devoirs. Annabelle est sympa, patiente et amusante. J'aime beaucoup être avec elle. C'est super d'avoir une meilleure amie qu'on voit tous les jours, pas vrai ?

De temps en temps, le weekend, il y a une fête d'anniversaire chez une copine ou chez un copain. J'adore retrouver mes amis pour une boum avec de la bonne musique et de la bonne nourriture. Les copains et les copines de mon âge partagent mes goûts et me comprennent bien. C'est super !

A +

Suzie

Tips to students

- Be sure to open and close your message appropriately.
- Explain where you live and how old you are.
- Show curiosity and interest in what your friend says. Ask some questions aimed at clarifications and details.
- Use paragraphs, transitions, interjections and a variety of nouns, verbs, adjectives and adverbs.
- Note similarities and differences between your interactions with friends and those of your pen pal's with his/her friends.

Tips to teachers

- Remind students opening and closing terms like **Cher/Chère** and **A+/A bientôt, Salut** etc.
- Be sure to monitor the writing of students. Have them to edit their work
- Encourage students to use what they already know. Teach them to paraphrase!
- Remind students to use coordinating conjunctions like **mais**, interjections like **Crois-moi**, question words like **Pourquoi** as well as transitional words and phrases such as *C'est pourquoi*.
- Encourage students to express opinions using expressions such as **A mon avis** or **Je pense que**.
- Encourage students to explain and expand their thinking with compound sentences using terms such as **parce que** and **car**.
- Encourage students to note differences.
- Review interrogative structures (pitch of voice and *est-ce que* methods for informal register)
- Review present, near future and passé composé tenses
- Give students the list of *Tips to students* as a rubric and hold them accountable.

E. Presentational communication activities

Written: an e-mail to someone close to you (brother, sister, uncle, aunt…)

Topic/context: le rôle des amis dans la vie des adolescents

Ecrivez un courriel à un membre de la famille. Parlez de vos amis, décrivez-en un ou deux, dites pourquoi vous les aimez bien et pourquoi ils jouent un rôle important dans votre vie.

- description de l'ami(e)
- ses qualités
- vos similarités et vos différences
- ce que vous faites ensemble

Oral: recording

Topic/context: les amis, mode d'emploi

Enregistrez une présentation orale (ou faites un petit film) dans lequel vous parlez de l'importance des amis et d'une « amitié réussie ». Que faut-il faire pour établir et maintenir une belle amitié ?

Oral or written: visual Interpretation

Instructions for a visual interpretation exercise based on the photo of a teenager from a Francophone region texting friends.

Décrivez la photo: quoi, qui, quel âge, où, à quelle heure. Décrivez surtout l'activité et imaginez un contexte. Exprimez des opinions.

Oral or written: Cultural comparison

Instructions for a cultural comparison exercise based on the previous photo and the photo of an American teenager involved in a similar or different activity.

Comparez les deux photos: quoi, qui, quel âge, où, à quelle heure. Exprimez des opinions sur les similitudes et les différences.

F. Projects

The following activities allow students to engage in research or reflection and practice written and oral presentational skills.

1. Formative activity (the activity has to be written and edited, as well as practiced orally)

- Choisissez une de vos activités les plus fréquentes avec un(e) ami(e) ou avec des amis. Avec un(e) camarade de classe, composez un petit **dialogue** entre vous en français et enregistrez-le sur Google Voice ou faites une vidéo sur You Tube.

- Faites un **sondage** parmi 6 de vos amis au sujet de leurs activités favorites avec leurs amis. Montrez les résultats graphiquement dans un tableau et expliquez-les oralement.

2. Summative activity (une réflexion)

Dans un premier temps, décrivez l'idéal du/de la meilleur(e) ami(e). Dans un deuxième temps, expliquez la dynamique des relations entre adolescents. Dans un troisième temps, décrivez vos activités avec des amis et leurs effets sur votre joie de vivre et votre attitude. Faites attention d'inclure les choses suivantes :

- Un petit essai de réflexion
- Trois parties bien développées (la description d'un(e) ami(e), la dynamique des relations entre amis, les activités communes et leurs effets)
- Des détails de description et des opinions
- Le présent, le passé composé et le futur proche d'une variété de verbes
- Un bon mélange de phrases composées et simples
- Des adjectifs, des adverbes et des mots charnières

Exemple de critères de notation

1. Le sujet est bien développé.

2. Les verbes sont bien conjugués.

3. Les phrases sont complètes, cohérentes et parfois complexes.

4. Il y a une variété de vocabulaire (noms, verbes et aussi des adjectifs, des adverbes et des mots-charnières).

5. La présentation est propre, clairement organisée et soignée. Les conventions sont respectées (ponctuation etc.).

Level 2 - Unit 3

Eating/Manger

> *The 3 modes of communication*
>
> - *Interpretive (print, visual and audio-visual)*
> - *Interpersonal (writing and speaking to one another)*
> - *Presentational (oral and written)*

Theme: (AP)Global Challenges/(DP)Global Issues and Health

A. Performance Objectives

- Interpret short authentic passages that are in the target language [print, audio, audio-visual] and that are related to food, in parts of the francophone world.

- Describe and discuss meals, shopping for food and eating habits in the interpersonal and presentational modes of communication.

B. Essential Questions

1. **Comment mange-t-on sainement? Est-ce une question de budget?**

2. **Faut-il vivre pour manger ou manger pour vivre?**

Inquiry statement: Pour être et rester en bonne santé physique et mentale, il faut manger de façon saine et équilibrée sans autant se priver de petites gâteries.

C. Interpretive communication activities

1. Reading-group and individual with authentic print resources [text/text with pictures]

2. Listening: to the instructor and/or peers

3. Listening to authentic audio/audio-visual material [simple news, videos, songs, movie excerpts etc.]

D. Interpersonal communication activities

1. Speaking - paired activity

➤ **Prompts, instructions and tips for a guided conversation**

Parlez avec un(e) camarade de classe de ce que vous mangez habituellement.	Parlez avec un(e) camarade de classe d'un plat spécial dans votre famille.
• *vos repas à la maison* • *vos goûters et vos en-cas* • *la valeur nutritionnelle et l'équilibre dans votre régime*	• *à quelle occasion* • *ses origines* • *les ingrédients ou la recette* • *la présentation*

Tips to students	Tips to teachers
• Be sure to listen carefully to your friends and react to what they say either by answering questions they pose or interjecting surprise, regret, happiness etc. • Ask for clarification by posing direct questions or repeating what you may have understood. • Ask for details [with question words such as *comment, pourquoi, quand, avec qui, où,* or with adverbs such as *souvent, régulièrement, jamais* etc.]. • Use transitions that make sense in the context. String your sentences logically with the appropriate *mot charnière*. Do not jump to another topic without a logical reason for it. • Show curiosity and interest in what your friend says. *Compare what they do with what you do.* • Make suggestions and express opinions. Justify them.	• Be sure to monitor the various pairs of students and give them feedback. • Encourage students to use what they already know. Teach them to paraphrase. • Encourage students to make frequent use of transitional words or phrases such as *alors, ainsi, ensuite, c'est pourquoi, c'est parce que, quand même, donc* etc. • Teach students to use coordinating conjunctions like mais, et, car, parce que as well as interjections like Vraiment, Pas possible, Tu blagues and question words like Qui, Comment, Quand, Pourquoi, Tu peux me dire. All these will allow students to provide and ask for details. • Teach students vocabulary necessary to express opinions such as *Moi, je pense que, A mon avis, Selon moi, Je crois que, je suis sûr(e) que* • Teach students vocabulary necessary to give advice such as *Tu peux peut-être + infinitive, Je te conseille de + infinitive, J'espère que…* • Remind students to use adjectives and adverbs to enrich their sentences.

2. Writing - answering an e-mail

Prompt, instructions and tips for an e-mail response

> ➢ **Répondez au courriel de votre correspondant. Répondez à ses questions et posez-lui aussi deux questions.**

Cher Marc,

La dernière fois que je t'ai écrit, je t'ai parlé de mes amis. Aujourd'hui, je voudrais t'expliquer un peu comment nous mangeons pendant la semaine, ici en Belgique.

Le matin, je mange généralement des gaufres au petit déjeuner, avec un verre de jus d'orange. A midi, si je mange à l'école, je vais à la cantine et je mange un plat complet comme du poulet avec des frites, une salade verte, un petit fromage et un fruit. Quelquefois, avec des copains, on va chez le boulanger pour acheter un sandwich et on va le manger au parc.

Quand je rentre de l'école, j'ai souvent un pain au chocolat ou quelques chips comme goûter avec un verre de lait ou du lait au chocolat. Notre dîner en famille est vers 20h et on mange une soupe, un peu de charcuterie et un légume.

Je voudrais savoir comment ça se passe chez toi. J'ai entendu dire que les Américains mangent toute la journée et à n'importe quelle heure. C'est vrai ?

A un de ces jours,

François

Tips to students

- Be sure to open and close your message appropriately.
- Explain where you live and how old you are.
- Show curiosity and interest in what your friend says. Ask some questions aimed at clarifications and details.
- Use paragraphs, transitions, interjections and a variety of nouns, verbs, adjectives and adverbs.
- Note similarities and differences between your interactions with friends and those of your pen pal's with his/her friends.

Tips to teachers

- Remind students opening and closing terms like **Cher/Chère, A+/A bientôt, Salut** etc.
- Be sure to monitor the writing of students. Have them to edit their work
- Encourage students to use what they already know. Teach them to paraphrase!
- Remind students to use coordinating conjunctions like **mais**, interjections like **Crois-moi, Tiens** or **Dis donc**, question words like **Pourquoi donc** as well as transitional words and phrases such as *Voilà pourquoi, Mais quand même as well as impersonal expressions such as **Il est certain que, Il faut dire que, Il est bon de***.
- Encourage students to express opinions using expressions such as **A mon avis** or **Je pense que** (and perhaps ask questions starting with **Selon toi**).
- Encourage students to explain and expand their thinking with compound sentences using terms such as **parce que** and **car**.
- Encourage students to note differences. Teach them the phrases **tandis que** and **alors que**.
- Review interrogative structures (pitch of voice and *est-ce que* methods for informal register)
- Review present, near future and passé composé tenses
- Give students the list of *Tips to students* as a rubric and hold them accountable.

E. Presentational communication activities

Written: graph and menu options

1. Faites un tableau qui indique ce que vous mangez le plus fréquemment un jour de semaine et aussi le weekend. Vous pouvez modifier le tableau suivant si vous voulez.

	Au petit déjeuner	Au déjeuner	Un goûter	Au dîner
Lundi				
Dimanche				

2. Composez un menu pour le dîner de dimanche soir. Présentez-le comme le menu que vous recevez par exemple à un mariage (petit poster).

Oral: recording

Faites un enregistrement oral ou audio-visuel pour votre classe. Expliquez comment il faut manger pour être en bonne santé. Faites attention aux formes verbales de l'impératif puisque vous vous adressez à l'ensemble de vos camarades.

Oral or written: visual Interpretation

Instructions for a visual interpretation exercise based on the photo of a French family making crepes.
Décrivez la photo: qui, quoi, où, ce qu'ils font, à quelle occasion. Exprimez des opinions et imaginez une situation précise.

Oral or written: Cultural comparison

Instructions for a cultural comparison exercise based on the previous photo and the photo of an American family having breakfast in a restaurant.
Comparez les deux photos. Exprimez des opinions sur les similitudes et les différences.

F. Projects

The following activities allow students to engage in research, reflection and creative activities while *practicing written and oral presentational skills.*

1. Formative activity (the activity has to be written and edited, as well as practiced orally)

- Composez une petite scène de café en français et enregistrez-la sur Google Voice ou faites une vidéo sur You Tube.

- Faites un sondage parmi 6 de vos amis au sujet de leurs petits déjeuners, leurs déjeuners ou leurs dîners favoris. Montrez les résultats graphiquement dans un tableau.

2. Summative activity (oral or written)

Dans un premier temps, parlez de ce qu'il faut manger pour rester en bonne santé. Dans un deuxième temps, parlez de choses que vous mangez simplement pour vous faire plaisir. Dans un troisième temps, faites une petite réflexion concernant ce que vous pouvez faire pour manger plus sainement. Faites attention d'inclure les choses suivantes:

- Le format d'un petit essai
- Trois parties bien développées (une pour la nourriture qui est bonne pour la santé, une autre pour les « gâteries » et une dernière pour des réflexions).
- Des détails de description et des opinions
- Le présent, le passé composé et le futur proche d'une variété de verbes
- Un bon mélange de phrases composées et simples
- Des adjectifs, des adverbes et des mots charnières

Exemple de critères de notation

1. Le sujet est bien développé.

2. Les verbes sont bien conjugués.

3. Les phrases sont complètes, cohérentes et parfois complexes.

4. Il y a une variété de vocabulaire (noms, verbes et aussi des adjectifs, des adverbes et des mots-charnières).

5. La présentation est propre, clairement organisée et soignée. Les conventions sont respectées (ponctuation etc.).

Level 2 - Unit 4

Les Sports/Sports

The 3 modes of communication

- *Interpretive (print, visual and audio-visual)*
- *Interpersonal (writing and speaking to one another)*
- *Presentational (oral and written)*

Theme: (AP)Global Challenges/(DP)Health and Leisure

A. Performance Objectives

- Interpret short authentic passages that are in the target language [print, audio, audio-visual] and that are related to sports in parts of the francophone world.

- Describe and discuss sports in the interpersonal and presentational modes of communication.

B. Essential Questions

1. **Pourquoi le sport est-il important dans la vie des jeunes partout dans le monde?**

2. **Dans quelle mesure le sport est-il plutôt un loisir ou une forme de compétition?**

Inquiry statement: Les sports les plus populaires varient parfois d'une culture à l'autre mais on peut dire avec certitude qu'ils représentent plus que les meilleurs efforts de l'athlète; les sports sont parfois le chemin à la gloire et à la fortune.

C. Interpretive communication activities

1. Reading-group and individual with authentic print resources [text/text with pictures]

2. Listening: to the instructor and/or peers

3. Listening to authentic audio/audio-visual material [simple news, videos, songs, movie excerpts etc.]

D. Interpersonal communication activities

1. Speaking - paired activity

> ## Prompts, instructions and tips for a guided conversation

Parlez avec un(e) camarade de classe de vos sports préférés.	Parlez avec un(e) camarade de classe d'un(e) athlète que vous admirez.
• *vous suivez les sports à la télévision ou en personne ?* • *vous regardez avec des amis ou la famille* • *vous faites des sports individuels ? d'équipe ?*	• *quel sport* • *les caractéristiques de ce sport* • *quelle équipe* • *les caractéristiques de l'athlète*

Tips to students	*Tips to teachers*
• *Be sure to listen carefully to your friends and react to what they say either by answering questions they pose or interjecting surprise, regret, happiness etc.* • *Ask for clarification by posing direct questions or repeating what you may have understood.* • *Ask for details [with question words such as **comment, pourquoi, quand, avec qui, où**, or with adverbs such as **souvent, régulièrement, jamais** etc.].* • *Use transitions that make sense in the context. String your sentences logically with the appropriate mot charnière. Do not jump to another topic without a logical reason for it.* • *Show curiosity and interest in what your friend says. Compare what they do with what you do.* • *Make suggestions and express opinions. Justify them.*	• *Be sure to monitor the various pairs of students and give them feedback.* • *Encourage students to use what they already know. Teach them to paraphrase.* • *Encourage students to make frequent use of transitional words or phrases such as **alors, ainsi, ensuite, c'est pourquoi, c'est parce que, quand même, donc** etc.* • *Teach students to use coordinating conjunctions like **mais, et, car, parce que** as well as interjections like **Vraiment, Pas possible, Tu blagues** and question words like **Qui, Comment, Quand, Pourquoi, Tu peux me dire**. All these will allow students to provide and ask for details.* • *Teach students vocabulary necessary to express opinions such as **Moi, je pense que, A mon avis, Selon moi, Je crois que, je suis sûr(e) que*** • *Teach students vocabulary necessary to give advice such as **Tu peux peut-être** + infinitive, **Je te conseille de** + infinitive, **J'espère que**…* • *Remind students to use adjectives and adverbs to enrich their sentences.*

2. Writing - answering an e-mail

Prompt, instructions and tips for an e-mail response

> ➤ **Répondez au courriel de vos parents. Répondez à leurs questions et posez-leur aussi deux questions.**

Chère Denise,

Tu nous manques beaucoup. J'espère que tout va bien pour toi dans ta famille d'accueil.

Aujourd'hui, nous nous sommes inscrits à une session d'apprentissage de kayak. Nous commençons demain. D'abord nous allons faire des circuits assez courts sur la rivière. Eventuellement nous allons pouvoir participer à des excursions plus ambitieuses sur des rivières et des fleuves de montagne avec des rapides et de petites chutes. Nous nous réjouissons d'avance.

Ta tante Joëlle faisait partie d/un club de kayak quand nous étions jeunes et elle participait même à des compétitions. Tiens, je me demande si un jour nous allons pouvoir lui faire la compétition ?

Je pense qu'en France, le sport au lycée se limite à quelques activités de plein air comme jouer au foot et faire de la gymnastique. Alors beaucoup de jeunes sont membres de clubs sportifs. Est-ce que c'est comme ça dans ton école d'échange ?

Nous attendons ta réponse avec beaucoup d'impatience. Réponds vite !

Grosses bises,

Maman et papa

Tips to students

- Be sure to open and close your message appropriately.
- Use the appropriate verbal forms when addressing both parents.
- Respond to questions. Ask some of your own questions aimed at clarifications and details.
- Use paragraphs, transitions, interjections and a variety of nouns, verbs, adjectives and adverbs.
- Use the verbal tense that is appropriate for your response regardless of the tenses found in the message to you.
- Acknowledge or deny differences between Americans and French regarding the role of sports in schools.

Tips to teachers

- Remind students opening and closing terms like **Chers, A+/A bientôt, Salut** etc.
- Teach students terms of endearment such as **Bises, Bisous** and **Je vous embrasse**.
- Be sure to monitor the writing of students. Have them to edit their work
- Encourage students to use what they already know. Teach them to paraphrase!
- Remind students to use coordinating conjunctions like **mais**, interjections like **Crois-moi, Tiens** or **Dis donc**, question words like **Pourquoi donc** as well as transitional words and phrases such as *Voilà pourquoi, Mais quand même as well as impersonal expressions such as Il est certain que, Il faut dire que, Il est bon de*.
- Encourage students to express opinions using expressions such as **A mon avis** or **Je pense que** (and perhaps ask questions starting with **Selon toi**).
- Encourage students to explain and expand their thinking with compound sentences using terms such as **parce que** and **car**.
- Encourage students to note differences. Teach them the phrases **tandis que** and **alors que**.
- Review interrogative structures (pitch of voice and *est-ce que* methods for informal register)
- Review present, near future and passé composé tenses. Introduce *imparfait*.
- Review reflexive structures.
- Give students the list of *Tips to students* as a rubric and hold them accountable

E. Presentational communication activities

Written: graph and guide options

1. Faites un tableau qui indique vos activités de la semaine et du weekend. Parlez surtout de votre routine, de votre toilette et de vos activités physiques. Vous pouvez modifier le tableau suivant si vous voulez.

	Avant l'école	A l'école	Après l'école
Lundi			
Samedi/Dimanche			

2. Qu'avez-vous fait récemment et régulièrement et que comptez-vous faire dans le proche avenir pour être et rester en bonne forme (petit guide sur poster ou petite vidéo).

Oral: recording

Faites un enregistrement oral ou audio-visuel pour votre classe. Il faut **convaincre** vos camarades que l'activité physique est essentielle pour être en bonne santé. Vous pouvez utiliser des verbes à l'impératif mais faites attention aux formes verbales puisque vous vous adressez à l'ensemble de vos camarades. Vous pouvez aussi faire une liste de conseils avec des verbes à l'infinitif.

Oral or written: visual Interpretation

Instructions for a visual interpretation exercise based on the photo of Francophone teenagers involved in a sports or physical activity
Décrivez la photo: qui, quoi, où, ce qu'ils font. Exprimez des opinions.

Oral or written: cultural comparison

Instructions for a cultural comparison exercise based on the previous photo and the photo of American teenagers involved in sports or physical activity.
Comparez les deux photos. Exprimez des opinions sur les similitudes et les différences.

F. Projects

The following activities allow students to engage in research, reflection and creative activities while practicing written and oral presentational skills.

1. Formative activity (the activity has to be written and edited, as well as practiced orally)

- Créez une publicité pour une séance d'activité physique et enregistrez-la sur Google Voice ou faites une vidéo sur You Tube.

- Faites un sondage parmi 6 de vos amis au sujet de leurs activités physiques favorites (marche, promenade, escalade, cyclisme, sports d'équipe et sports individuels). Montrez les résultats graphiquement dans un tableau.

2. Summative activity (oral or written)

Vous préparez un petit discours à un groupe de jeunes collégiens ; vous allez leur parler de ce qu'il faut faire pour rester en bonne santé physique. Parlez des avantages de l'activité physique mais donnez aussi des conseils de précaution. Faites attention d'inclure les choses suivantes :

- Le format d'un discours à des élèves plus jeunes
- Des exemples d'activités physiques
- Des détails et des opinions
- Deux parties bien développées (les activités favorables à la bonne santé, l'autre pour les conseils).
- Le présent, l'impératif, l'infinitif et le futur proche d'une variété de verbes
- Un bon mélange de phrases composées et simples
- Des adjectifs, des adverbes et des mots charnières

Exemple de critères de notation

1. Le sujet est bien développé.

2. Les verbes sont bien conjugués et le registre est approprié.

3. Les phrases sont complètes, cohérentes et parfois complexes.

4. Il y a une variété de vocabulaire (des noms, des verbes et aussi des adjectifs, des adverbes et des mots-charnières).

5. La présentation est clairement organisée et compréhensible.

Level 2 - Unit 5

La télévision et le cinéma/Television and Cinema

> *The 3 modes of communication*
>
> - *Interpretive (print, visual and audio-visual)*
> - *Interpersonal (writing and speaking to one another)*
> - *Presentational (oral and written)*

Theme: (AP)La technologie/(DP)Communication and Media

A. Performance Objectives

- Interpret short authentic passages that are in the target language [print *[with or without image]*, audio, audio-visual] and that are related to television and cinema in parts of the francophone world.

- Describe and discuss sports in the interpersonal and presentational modes of communication.

B. Essential Questions

1. **Quel est l'avenir de la télévision et du cinéma dans le monde actuel?**

2. **Comment la télévision et le cinéma sont-ils impactés par la technologie moderne?**

Statement of inquiry: La télévision et le cinéma jouent des rôles multiples dans les sociétés modernes; divertissement, information et éducation, publicité, propagande, outil de mondialisation.

C. Interpretive communication activities

1. Reading-group and individual with authentic print resources [text/text with pictures]

2. Listening: to the instructor and/or peers

3. Listening to authentic audio/audio-visual material [simple news, videos, songs, movie excerpts etc.]

D. Interpersonal communication activities

1. Speaking - paired activity

> **Prompts, instructions and tips for a guided conversation**

Parlez avec un(e) camarade de classe du rôle de la télé dans votre vie.	Parlez avec un(e) camarade de classe du rôle du cinéma dans votre vie.
• *quand et avec qui regardez-vous la télé ? discutez-vous ?* • *qu'est-ce que vous regardez ?* • *mangez-vous pendant le visionnement ?*	• *quel type de films aimez-vous?* • *quand, où, avec qui allez-vous au cinéma?* • *quelles sont vos vedettes favorites ?* • *suivez-vous vos vedettes sur Twitter?*

Tips to students	*Tips to teachers*
• *Be sure to listen carefully to your friends and react to what they say either by answering questions they pose or interjecting surprise, regret, happiness etc.* • *Ask for clarification by posing direct questions or repeating what you may have understood.* • *Ask for details [with question words such as **comment, pourquoi, quand, avec qui, où**, or with adverbs such as **souvent, régulièrement, jamais** etc.].* • *Use transitions that make sense in the context. String your sentences logically with the appropriate mot charnière. Do not jump to another topic without a logical reason for it.* • *Show curiosity and interest in what your friend says. Compare what they do with what you do.* • *Make suggestions and express opinions. Justify them.*	• *Be sure to monitor the various pairs of students and give them feedback.* • *Encourage students to use what they already know. Teach them to paraphrase.* • *Encourage students to make frequent use of transitional words or phrases such as **alors, ainsi, ensuite, c'est pourquoi, c'est parce que, quand même, donc** etc.* • *Teach students to use coordinating conjunctions like **mais, et, car, parce que** as well as interjections like **Vraiment, Pas possible, Tu blagues** and question words like **Qui, Comment, Quand, Pourquoi, Tu peux me dire**. All these will allow students to provide and ask for details.* • *Teach students vocabulary necessary to express opinions such as **Moi, je pense que, A mon avis, Selon moi, Je crois que, je suis sûr(e) que*** • *Teach students vocabulary necessary to give advice such as **Tu peux peut-être** + **infinitive, Je te conseille de** + **infinitive*** • *Remind students to use adjectives and adverbs to enrich their sentences.*

2. Writing - answering an e-mail

Prompt, instructions and tips for an e-mail response

> ➢ **Répondez au courriel de vos correspondants. Répondez à leurs questions et posez-leur aussi deux questions.**

Cher Jean-Luc,

Demain, c'est samedi et notre cours de maths a été annulé parce que le professeur est malade. Alors nous allons faire une ballade en bicyclette avec des copains. Comme nous n'habitons pas très loin de Giverny, nous allons nous y arrêter et y pique-niquer. Nous avons déjà préparé nos sandwichs pour le déjeuner, un casse-croûte pour l'après-midi et, naturellement, quelques bouteilles d'eau.

Dimanche, on compte aller voir la première du dernier film de la série « The Hobbit ». Nous nous réjouissons d'avance parce que nous avons lu tous les livres et vu les deux premiers films que nous avons adorés. Le film est déjà sorti aux États-Unis ? Tu l'as vu ?

Comme on n'a pas le temps de regarder la télé pendant la semaine, on aime bien aller au cinéma le weekend. On regarde tout de même quelquefois certaines émissions sur le net. Quand on fait ça, on envoie généralement des texto à des copains et on discute ce qu'on visionne.

Et toi, qu'est-ce que tu aimes regarder à la télé ou au ciné ? Qu'est-ce que tu en penses ?

Tes jumeaux favoris,

Jérémy et Thomas

Tips to students

- Be sure to open and close your message appropriately.
- Use the appropriate verbal forms when addressing the two boys.
- Respond to questions. Ask some of your own questions aimed at clarifications and details.
- Use paragraphs, transitions, interjections and a variety of nouns, verbs, adjectives and adverbs.
- Use the verbal tense that is appropriate for your response regardless of the tenses found in the message to you.
- Confirm or deny differences between Americans and French adolescents regarding the role of TV and cinema.

Tips to teachers

- Remind students opening and closing terms like **Chers, A+/A bientôt, Salut** etc.
- Be sure to monitor the writing of students. Have them to edit their work
- Encourage students to use what they already know. Teach them to paraphrase!
- Remind students to use coordinating conjunctions like **mais**, interjections like **Crois-moi, Tiens** or **Dis donc**, question words like **Pourquoi donc** as well as transitional words and phrases such as *Voilà pourquoi, Mais quand même as well as impersonal expressions such as **Il est certain que, Il faut dire que, Il est bon de***.
- Encourage students to express opinions using expressions such as **A mon avis** or **Je pense que** (and perhaps ask questions starting with **Selon toi**).
- Encourage students to explain and expand their thinking with compound sentences using terms such as **parce que** and **car**.
- Encourage students to note differences. Teach them the phrases **tandis que** and **alors que**.
- Review interrogative structures (pitch of voice and *est-ce que* methods for informal register)
- Review the use of *on* instead of *nous* in familiar conversations.
- Review present, near future and passé composé tenses. Review reflexive structures.
- Give students the list of *Tips to students* as a rubric and hold them accountable.

E. Presentational communication activities

Written: graph and advertisement options

1. Faites un tableau qui indique ce que vous regardez (à la télé ou sur le net) le plus fréquemment un jour de semaine et aussi le weekend. Vous pouvez modifier le tableau suivant si vous voulez.

	Jeux	Emissions de sport	Informations/Actualités	Séries/Feuilletons
En semaine				
Le weekend				

2. Créez le texte illustré d'une **bande-annonce** pour un film qui va sortir bientôt au cinéma.

Oral: recording

Faites la critique d'un film pour une annonce à vos camarades de lycée. Expliquez-leur pourquoi ils doivent ou ne doivent pas aller voir un certain film que vous venez de voir au cinéma.

Oral or written: visual Interpretation

*Instructions for a visual interpretation exercise based on a **bande-annonce** (Francophone region)*

Décrivez la bande-annonce: qui, quoi, où, action, genre, acteurs/actrices, réalisateur/réalisatrice etc. Exprimez des opinions.

Oral or written: cultural comparison

Instructions for a cultural comparison exercise based on the previous bande-annonce and an American bande-annonce
Comparez les deux. Exprimez des opinions sur les similitudes et les différences.

F. Projects

The following activities allow students to engage in research, reflection and creative activities while *practicing written and oral presentational skills.*

1. Formative activity (the activity has to be written and edited, as well as practiced orally)

- Avec un ou une camarade, discutez en français d'un film ou d'un épisode de feuilleton que vous avez vu. Enregistrez la conversation sur Google Voice ou sur un magnétophone digital.

- Faites un sondage parmi 6 de vos amis au sujet de a) ce qu'ils aiment visionner et b) leurs méthodes favorites de visionner (télé, internet, cinéma, SmartPhone etc.). Montrez les résultats graphiquement dans un tableau.

2. Summative activity (oral or written)

Vous allez parler à un groupe de jeunes francophones du rôle de la télé et du cinéma dans votre vie. Dans un premier temps, parlez de ce que vous aimez voir sur un grand ou petit écran. Dans un deuxième temps, comparez avec ce que vos parents aiment visionner. Tâchez d'inclure les choses suivantes :

- Votre méthode de visionnement préférée
- Des exemples d'émission et de film que vous aimez (et pourquoi)
- La méthode de visionnement préférée de vos parents
- Une émission préférée de vos parents et ce que vous en pensez
- Le présent, le passé composé, l'imparfait et le futur proche d'une variété de verbes
- Un bon mélange de phrases composées et simples
- Des adjectifs, des adverbes et des mots charnières

Exemple de critères de notation

1. Le sujet est bien développé.

2. Les verbes sont bien conjugués et le registre est approprié.

3. Les phrases sont complètes, cohérentes et parfois complexes.

4. Il y a une variété de vocabulaire (des noms, des verbes et aussi des adjectifs, des adverbes et des mots-charnières).

5. La présentation est clairement organisée et compréhensible.

LA FAMILLE ET LES AMIS

LA VIE DE TOUS LES JOURS

LA VIE URBAINE

LES LOISIRS ET LES PASSE-TEMPS

CHEZ MOI A LA MAISON

L'IDENTITÉ

LA DYNAMIQUE SOCIALE DE L'ADOLESCENT

Une super soirée

Le centre socio-éducatif Les Pel'tiots et la Fédération familles de France de la Moselle ont organisé leur soirée dansante tant attendue par les pré-ados et ados à la salle des fêtes. Pas moins de quatre-vingts participants, tous invités par le centre ou par les jeunes organisateurs, se sont retrouvés sous les projecteurs et la musique de RPL animation, encadrés par l'équipe d'animation et les bénévoles du CSE. Pour certains jeunes, cette soirée était leur première et ils comptent bien revenir à la prochaine, tant la bonne ambiance était au rendez-vous.

MANGER

LES SPORTS

LA TÉLÉVISION ET LE CINÉMA

Bande annonce

85866411R00044

Made in the USA
San Bernardino, CA
23 August 2018